Sai Chalisa

Published in Sanskriti Press
Rupa Publications India Pvt. Ltd 2025
7/16, Ansari Road, Daryaganj
New Delhi 110002

Sales centres:
Bengaluru Chennai
Hyderabad Jaipur Kathmandu
Kolkata Mumbai Prayagraj

Copyright © Rupa Publications India Pvt. Ltd 2025

All rights reserved.
No part of this publication may be reproduced, transmitted,
or stored in a retrieval system, in any form or by any means,
electronic, mechanical, photocopying, recording or otherwise,
without the prior permission of the publisher.

P-ISBN: 978-93-7003-740-3
E-ISBN: 978-93-7003-628-4

First impression 2025

10 9 8 7 6 5 4 3 2 1

Printed in India

This book is sold subject to the condition that it shall not, by way of
trade or otherwise, be lent, resold, hired out, or otherwise circulated,
without the publisher's prior consent, in any form of binding or
cover other than that in which it is published.

Contents

Introduction / 5

Chalisa / 9

श्री साईं बाबा आरती / 113

Shri Sai Baba Aarti / 116

Introduction

The *Sai Chalisa* is a revered devotional hymn dedicated to the beloved saint, Sai Baba of Shirdi, a symbol of compassion, spiritual wisdom, and divine grace. Composed in deep reverence for Sai Baba, the Chalisa extols his virtues and miraculous powers, which, according to his devotees, can transform lives and offer solace to the troubled soul. Sai Baba, who lived in Shirdi in the late 19th and early 20th centuries, is venerated as a saint who bridged the gap between different faiths and emphasized the importance of love, service, and devotion to God. Through its verses, the *Sai Chalisa* offers prayers for protection, healing, and spiritual upliftment, invoking Sai

Baba's blessings for peace and prosperity.

Structured in the traditional forty-verse format, the *Sai Chalisa* intricately describes the divine qualities of Sai Baba, his acts of kindness, and the miracles he performed to alleviate suffering. The lyrics of the Chalisa evoke a deep sense of reverence, reflecting the belief that Sai Baba's presence can bring spiritual enlightenment, eradicate pain, and guide the devotee towards the path of righteousness. Each verse serves as a powerful reminder of Sai Baba's unconditional love, which transcends religious boundaries and offers healing to all who seek his grace.

The tone of the *Sai Chalisa* is profoundly spiritual, filled with deep adoration and a sense of surrender to Sai Baba's divine will. The words flow with devotion, inviting the devotee to experience peace and contentment through faith and reliance on Sai Baba's guidance. Recited with unwavering devotion, the *Sai*

Chalisa holds the promise of inner peace, spiritual awakening, and divine protection. Whether performed during ritual worship or recited in moments of personal reflection, the *Sai Chalisa* becomes a powerful companion, leading the devotee to a deeper connection with the divine presence of Sai Baba. Through its verses, Sai Baba is not just a saint but a symbol of compassion, hope, and divine intervention in the lives of his followers.

Chalisa

श्री साईं के चरणों में, अपना शीश नवाऊं मैं
कैसे शिरडी साईं आए, सारा हाल सुनाऊं मैं

Shri Sai ke charanon mein,
apna sheesh navaun main
kaise Shirdi Sai aaye,
saara haal sunaoon main.

I humbly bow my head and surrender at the feet of Shri Sai Baba, our God; I explain how Shri Sai Baba had arrived at Shirdi.

कौन है माता, पिता कौन है, यह न किसी ने भी जाना
कहां जन्म साईं ने धारा, प्रश्न पहेली रहा बना

Kaun hai mata, pita kaun hai,
ye na kisi ne bhi jaana,
kahan janam sai ne dhaara,
prashna paheli raha bana.

No one knows who is the Mother and who is the Father of Shri Sai Baba. From the beginning, the details of where Shri Sai Baba was born have remained a mystery.

कोई कहे अयोध्या के, ये रामचन्द्र भगवान हैं
कोई कहता साईं बाबा, पवन-पुत्र हनुमान हैं

Koi kahe Ayodhya ke,
ye Ramchandra bhagwan hai,
koi kehta Sai baba,
pavan putra Hanuman hai.

Some say that Shri Sai Baba has come from Ayodhya (the birthplace of Lord Shri Rama). They also consider Him as another avatar (incarnation) of Lord Shri Rama. Some say that Shri Sai Baba is Lord Shri Hanuman, the son of Vayu (wind).

कोई कहता मंगल मूर्ति, श्री गजानन हैं साईं।
कोई कहता गोकुल-मोहन, देवकी नन्दन हैं साईं

Koi kehta mangal moorti,
Shri Gajanan hai Sai,
koi kehta Gokul Mohan,
Devki Nandan hain Sai.

Some persons say that Shri Sai Baba is the incarnation of Lord Ganesha, the auspicious Deity. Some persons say that Shri Sai Baba is the son of Devaki, Lord Krishna who was the love of Gokul, the place where Shri Krishna was brought up.

शंकर समझ भक्त कई तो, बाबा को भजते रहते
कोई कह अवतार दत्त का, पूजा साईं की करते

Shankar Samajh Bhakt kai to,
Baba ko bhajte rehte,
koi kahe avtar Datt ka,
pooja Sai ki karte.

The several devotees of Lord Shri Shankar (Lord Shiva) worship Shri Sai Baba identifying Him as Lord Shiva. Several others say that Shri Sai Baba is the avatar of Shri Dattatreya, the Lord of Yoga and First spiritual Guru. They perform prayers to Shri Sai Baba considering thus.

कुछ भी मानो उनको तुम, पर साईं हैं सच्चे भगवान
बड़े दयालु, दीनबन्धु, कितनों को दिया जीवनदान

Kuch bhi maano unko tum,
par Sai hai sacche bhagwan
bade dayalu deen bandhu,
kitnon ko diya jeevandaan.

Irrespective of what you consider or believe him to be, Shri Sai Baba is the true God. He is very benevolent and is close to poor and downtrodden. He has blessed life to innumerable persons.

कई बरस पहले की घटना, तुम्हें सुनाऊंगा मैं बात
किसी भाग्यशाली की शिरडी में, आई थी बारात

Kai baras pehle ki ghatna,
tumhein sunaunga main baat
kisee bhagyshaali ki,
Shirdi mein aayi thi baraat.

I will describe the details of an incident which happened long ago. Some person who had the utmost luck and the blessings had his wedding procession passing through Shirdi.

आया साथ उसी के था, बालक एक बहुत सुंदर
आया, आकर वहीं बस गया, पावन शिरडी किया नगर

Aaya saath usee ke tha,
balak ek bahut sundar
aaya aakr vahin bas gaya,
paavan Shirdi kiya nagar.

An extremely handsome young boy had come alongwith the marriage procession. On reaching Shirdi, he had decided to stay there and made Shirdi a holy and sacred place.

कई दिनों तक रहा भटकता, भिक्षा मांगी उसने दर-दर।
और दिखाई ऐसी लीला, जग में जो हो गई अमर

Kai dinon tak raha bhatakta,
bhiksha mangi usne dar-dar.
aur dikhai aisi leela,
jag mein jo ho gai amar.

That young boy was going around Shirdi. He took alms from door to door (like a sanyasi seeking bhiksha—not possessing anything). He had also performed holy miracles. His glory was being discussed and spread eternally around the world.

जैसे-जैसे उमर बढ़ी, बढ़ती ही वैसे गई शान
घर-घर होने लगा नगर में, साईं बाबा का गुणगान

*Jaise-jaise umar badhi,
badhti hi vaise gayi shaan
ghar-ghar hone laga nagar mein,
Sai baba ka gungaan*

While that young boy was growing up, his popularity, fame and glory also were getting widespread. Every household in Shirdi had started chanting the good attributes of Shri Sai Baba.

दिग दिगन्त में लगा गूंजने, फिर तो साईं जी का नाम
दीन दुखी की रक्षा करना, यही रहा बाबा का काम

Dig digant mein laga goonjane,
phir to Sai ji ka naam
deen dukhi ki raksha karna,
yahi raha Baba ka kaam

All the directions and corners of the universe had vibrated with the echo emanating from the chants of Shri Sai Baba's name. The primary work of Shri Sai Baba is the protection of the poor & the downtrodden and alleviation of their pains.

बाबा के चरणों जाकर, जो कहता मैं हूं निर्धन
दया उसी पर होती उनकी, खुल जाते द:ख के बंधन

Baba ke charnon mein jaa kar,
jo kehta main hoon nirdhan
daya usi par hoti unki,
khul jaate dukh ke bandhan.

When an impoverished person seeks refuge in the holy feet of Shri Sai Baba, such poor person is blessed with kindness and benevolence. He is relieved of all the restraining ties of burden and pain.

कभी किसी ने मांगी भिक्षा, दो बाबा मुझको संतान।
एवं अस्तु तब कहकर साईं, देते थे उसको वरदान

*Kabhi kisi ne maangi bhiksha,
do baba mujhko santan.
Avem astu tab kehkar Sai,
dete the usko vardaan.*

Some other time, when a childless woman had asked Shri Sai Baba for a blessing of a child, Shri Sai Baba had said 'Avum Asthu' meaning 'let it happen' and blessed her with the boon.

स्वयं दु:खी बाबा हो जाते, दीन-दु:खी जन का हाल
अंत:करन भी साईं का, सागर जैसा रहा विशाल

*Swayam dukhee Baba ho jaate,
deen dukhi jan ka haal
antahkaran bhi Sai ka,
sagar jaisa raha vishal*

When Shri Sai Baba beholds the sight of the poor and sick people, He himself grieves. The holy soul of Shri Sai Baba is as vast and large as the ocean.

भक्त एक मद्रासी आया, घर का बहुत बड़ा धनवान
माल खजाना बेहद उसका, केवल नहीं रही संतान

Bhakt ek Madrasi aaya,
ghar ka bahut bada dhanwaan
Maal khajana behad uska,
keval nahi rahi santan

A devotee from South India who was wealthy, rich and prosperous had visited Shri Sai Baba. Though the said devotee had all the worldly treasures, he had lacked a child and had a longing for the same.

लगा मनाने साईंनाथ को, बाबा मुझ पर दया करो
झंझा से झंकृत नैया को, तुम ही मेरी पार करो

Laga manane Sainath ko,
Baba mujh par daya karo
jhanjha se jhankrit nayya ko,
tum meri paar karo

That childless rich man had begged for the kindness of Shri Sai Baba. He tried to convince Shri Sai Baba of his predicament. He told Shri Sai Baba that his life was a boat in turbulent and troubled waters and he sought Shri Sai Baba's help to come ashore.

कुलदीपक के बिना अंधेरा, छाया हुआ घर में मेरे
इसलिए आया हूं बाबा होकर शरनागत तेरे

Kuldeepak ke bina andhera,
chhaya hua ghar mein mere
isi liye aaya hoon Baba
hokar sharnagat tere

That childless rich man had said that without an heir to sustain the family's generations, there was darkness spreading at his home. He also said that he had come to Shri Sai Baba to offer himself unconditionally at the feet of Shri Sai Baba.

कुलदीपक के अभाव में, व्यर्थ है दौलत की माया
आज भिखारी बनकर बाबा, शरण तुम्हारी मैं आया

*Kuldeepak ke abhaav mein,
vyarth hai daulat ki maya
aaj bhikhari ban kar Baba,
sharan tumhari main aaya*

He had further said that his life is a wasteful existence in the absence of a progeny and that his wealth is meaningless. He ardently prayed, 'Shri Sai Baba, in spite of my wealth, I had come to you as a beggar; I have taken refuge at you, please help me.'

दे दे मुझको पुत्र दान, मैं ऋणी रहूंगा जीवन भर
और किसी की आस न मुझको, सिर्फ भरोसा है तुम पर

De de mujhko putra daan,
main rinee rahunga jeevan bhar
aur kisi ki aas na mujhko,
sirf bharosa hai tum par

He had further requested 'Shri Sai Baba, please bless me with a child. I will ever be indebted and grateful to you in my entire life. I do not have hope or faith in anyone else. I earnestly put my trust only in you.'

अनुनय-विनय बहुत की उसने, चरणों में धर के शीश
तब प्रसन्न होकर बाबा ने दिया भक्त को यह आशीष

Anunay-vianay bahut ki usne,
charanon mein dhar ke sheesh
tab prasann ho kar Baba ne
diya bhakt ko ye ashish

He had devoutly with all surrender and submission had prayed to Shri Sai Baba. He had bowed his head to the feet of Shri Sai Baba. Shri Sai Baba was convinced by the humility and the sincerity. Then He gave the said devotee this blessing.

अल्लाह भला करेगा तेरा, पुत्र जन्म हो तेरे घर
कृपा रहे तुम पर उसकी, और तेरे उस बालक पर

Allah bhala karaega tera,
putra janm ho tere ghar
kripa rahe tum par uski,
aur tere us baalak par

Allah shall do the good thing to you. A child shall be born at your home. God's kindness shall always be with you. The kindness shall also be with your child.

अब तक नहीं किसी ने पाया, साईं की कृपा का पार
पुत्र रतन दे मद्रासी को, धन्य किया उसका संसार

Ab tak nahi kisi ne paaya,
Sai ki kripa ka paar,
putra ratan de Madrasi ko,
dhanya kiya uska sansar

Till today, no person has ascertained anything which surpasses the kindness of Shri Sai Baba. By providing a gift of a child to the South Indian devotee, Shri Sai Baba had granted a magnificent boon to his life.

तन-मन से जो भजे उसी को, जग में होता है उद्धार
सांच को आंच नहीं है कोई, सदा झूठ की होती हार

Tan-man se jo bhaje usi ko,
jag mein hota uddhaar,
saanch ko aanch nahi hai koi,
sada jhooth ki hoti haar

Any person devoutly chanting the name of Shri Sai Baba always experiences all the benefits of this world. Truth is never faced with any kind of threat. Treachery and lies are always defeated.

मैं हूं सदा सहारे उसके, सदा रहूंगा उसका दास
साईं जैसा प्रभु मिला है, इतनी ही कम है क्या आद

Main hoon sada sahare uske,
sada rahunga uska das,
Sai jaisa prabhu mila hai,
itni hi kam hai kya aad

I live and survive because of the kindness and support of Shri Sai Baba. I shall always remain his ardent devotee and a servant. Shri Sai Baba is my God and I have found Him. This blessing itself is a tremendous faith and hope for me.

मेरा भी दिन था इक ऐसा, मिलती नहीं मुझे थी रोटी
तन पर कपड़ा दूर रहा था, शेष रही नन्ही सी लंगोटी

Mera bhi tha din ek aisa,
milti nahi mujhe thi roti,
tan par kapda door raha tha,
shesh rahi nanhi si langoti

I also had a phase like this once in my life whence I could not get any roti (food) to eat. On my body, I did not have good clothes to cover; I only had a meagre loin cloth (langoti—a piece of dhoti)

सरिता सन्मुख होने पर भी, मैं प्यासा का प्यासा था
दुर्दिन मेरा मेरे ऊपर, दावाग्नि बरसाता था

Sarita sanmukh hone par bhi,
main pyaa ka pyasa tha
durdin mera mere upar,
davgni barsata tha

The flowing river was in front of me. However, I had remained thirsty. My phase of misfortunes had showered upon me the miseries like flaming fires.

धरती के अतिरिक्त जगत में, मेरा कुछ अवलम्ब न था
बना भिखारी मैं दुनिया में, दर-दर ठोकर खाता था

Dharti ke atirikt jagat mein,
mera kuch avlambh na tha
bana bhikhari main duniya mein,
dar-dar thokar khata tha

In the whole of the universe, I had no place to take refuge except the land. I had become a seeker of alms in this world; I suffered from hurt and attacks from everywhere.

ऐसे में इक मित्र मिला जो, परम भक्त साईं का था
जंजालों से मुक्त, मगर इस, जगती में वह मुझसा था

Aise mein ek mitra mila jo,
param bhakt Sai ka tha
janjalon se mukt, magar iss,
jagati mein vah mujhsa tha

At such a situation, I had met a friend of mine; He was an ardent devotee of Shri Sai Baba. He was liberated of troubles in his life; However, the circumstances revealed that he was just like me.

बाबा के दर्शन के खातिर, मिल दोनों ने किया विचार
साईं जैसे दयामूर्ति के दर्शन को हो गए तैयार

Baba ke darshan ke khatir,
mil dono ne kiya vichaar,
Sai jaise dayamoorti ke,
darshan ko ho gaye tayyar

For the purpose of seeking and having the darshan of Shri Sai Baba, we (myself and my friend) thought, discussed and planned together. Shri Sai Baba is the embodiment of kindness and benevolence. We were ready for visiting Shri Sai Baba.

पावन शिरडी नगर में जाकर, देखी मतवाली मूर्ति
धन्य जन्म हो गया कि हमने, जब देखी साईं की सूरति

Paavan Shirdi nagar mein jaakar,
dekhi matwali moorti,
dhanya janam ho gaya ki humne,
jab dekhi Sai ki soorati

We went to the holy city of Shirdi and were blessed with the vision and darshan of Shri Sai Baba's idol. We were humbled that our birth and life were blessed the moment we beheld the vision of His divine appearance.

जबसे किये है दर्शन हमने, दुःख सारा काफूर हो गया
संकट सारे मिटे और, विपदाओं का अंत हो गया

Jabse kiye hai darshan humne,
dukh sara kafur ho gaya,
sankat sare mite aur,
vipdaon ka ant ho gaya

The moment we were blessed with the darshan of Shri Sai Baba, our sorrows had withered away. All our problems had disappeared and our hardships had ended.

मान और सम्मान मिला, भिक्षा में हमको बाबा से
प्रतिबिंबित हो उठे जगत में, हम साईं की आभा से

Maan aur sammaan mila,
bhiksha mein humko Baba se
prati bimbit ho uthe jagat me,
hum Sai ki aabha se

We were blessed and endowed with devotion and amazement with the darshan of Shri Sai Baba. This is the utmost benevolent endowment blessed by Shri Sai Baba.

बाबा ने सम्मान दिया है, मान दिया इस जीवन में
इसका ही सम्बल ले मैं, हंसता जाऊंगा जीवन में

Baba ne sammaan diya hai,
maan diya is jeevan mein,
iska hi sambhal le main,
hansta jaoonga jeevan me

Shri Sai Baba has granted us integrity, honor and esteem in our lives. We take refuge in His benevolent shelter of protection and shall be blessed and happy for the lifetime.

साईं की लीला का मेरे, मन पर ऐसा असर हुआ
लगता, जगती के कण-कण में, जैसे हो वह भरा हुआ

Sai ki leela ka mere,
mann par aisa asar hua
lagta, jagti ke kan-kan mein,
jaise ho vah bhara hua

The divinely blessed actions of Shri Sai Baba have tremendous impact in my thoughts. They guide my life. I can consciously understand that each and every place and space in this world is blessed with the greatness of Shri Sai Baba.

'काशीराम' बाबा का भक्त, इस शिरडी में रहता था
मैं साईं का साईं मेरा, वह दुनिया से कहता था

'Kashiram' baba ka bhakt,
iss Shirdi mein rehta tha,
main Sai ka, Sai mera,
vah duniya se kehta tha

Sri Kashiram was a passionate devotee of Shri Sai Baba. He was living in Shirdi. He used to recite to one and all in the universe as 'I belong to Shri Sai Baba and Shri Sai Baba belongs to me.'

सीकर स्वयं वस्त्र बेचता, ग्राम नगर बाजारों में
झंकृत उसकी हृदय तंत्री थी, साईं की झनकारों में

Seekar swayam vastra bechta,
gram nagar bajaron mein,
jhankrit uski hriday tantri thi,
Sai ki jhankaron mein

He was stitching the dresses and used to sell in the markets of the villages and cities. His heartbeats reverberated the divine voice of Shri Sai Baba.

स्तब्ध निशा थी, थे सोये, रजनी आंचल में चांद सितारे
नहीं सूझता रहा हाथ, को हाथ तिमिर के मारे

Stabdh nisha thi,
the soye aanchal mein chand sitare
nahin soojhta raha haath,
ko haath timir ke maare

Though the moon was shining and the stars were glittering, the night was very dark. The darkness was such that it was not possible to locate one hand from the other.

वस्त्र बेचकर लौट रहा था, हाय! हाट से काशी
विचित्र बड़ा संयोग कि उस दिन, आता था वह एकाकी

Vastra bech kar laut raha tha,
hai! haat se Kashi
vichitra bada sanyog ki us din,
aata tha vah ekaki

In that dark night, Sri Kashiram was back from the market after selling his garments. Astonishingly, he was quite alone and on his own.

घेर राह में खड़े हो गए, उसे कुटिल अन्यायी
मारो काटो लूटो इसको, ही ध्वनि पड़ी सुनाई

Gher rah mein khade ho gaye,
use kutil anyayi
maro kato looto isko,
hi dhvani padi sunai

In the pathway, he was suddenly stopped by a few persons who appeared deceitful and ruthless. Sri Kashiram could hear only word such as 'beat him, bash him, rob from him.'

लूट पीटकर उसे वहां से, कुटिल गये चम्पत हो
आघातों से मर्माहत हो, उसने दी थी संज्ञा खो

Loot peet kar use vahan se,
kutil gaye champat ho
aaghaaton se marmahat ho,
usne di thi sangya kho

The thieves had beaten up Sri Kashiram, looted from him and left the place. He had received severe injuries, wounds and lesions. Due to the severity, he had lost his consciousness.

बहुत देर तक पड़ा रहा वह, वहीं उसी हालत में
जाने कब कुछ होश हो उठा, उसको किसी पलक में

Bahut der tak pada raha vaha,
vahi usi haalat me
jaane kab kuch hosh utha,
usko kisi palak me

He was lying without consciousness for a very long time. After a long time, he had gradually recuperated without himself being aware of it.

अनजाने ही उसके मुंह से, निकल पड़ा था साईं
जिसकी प्रतिध्वनि शिर्डी में, बाबा को पड़ी सुनाई

Anjaane hi uske mooh se,
nikal pada tha Sai
jiki pratidhvani Shirdi me,
Baba ko padi sunai

He had blurted incoherently and even without his consciousness; he had recited the name of Shri Sai Baba. His appealing prayer voice had resounded in Shirdi; Shri Sai Baba had heard his ardent call for assistance.

क्षुब्ध उठा हो मानस उनका, बाबा गए विकल हो
लगता जैसे घटना सारी, घटी उन्हीं के सम्मुख हो

Khsubdh utha ho manas unka,
Baba gaye vikal ho
lagta jaise ghatna saari,
ghati unhi ke sammukh ho

Shri Sai Baba felt hurt in his heart and He was very much upset. It seemed that He could visualize the entire robbery and assault incident.

उन्मादी से इधर-उधर, तब बाबा लगे भटकने
सम्मुख चीजें जो भी आईं, उनको लगे पटकने

*Unmadi se idhar-udhar,
tab Baba lage bhatakne
sammukh cheezein jo bhi aai,
unko lage patakne*

The trouble faced by His devotee had upset Shri Sai Baba so much that He was anxiously striding in various directions with disturbed mind. His soul was so troubled and in His anxiety, He started tossing the things and objects which came in the way.

और धधकते अंगारों में, बाबा ने अपना कर डाला
हुए सशंकित सभी वहां, देख ताण्डव नृत्य निराला

Aur dhadhakte angaron mein,
Baba ne apna kar dala
huye sashankit sabhi vahan,
dekh tandav nritya nirala

To the shock of everyone present there, Shri Sai Baba had stepped on the red-hot scorching coal and the blazes. In His anger, he started dancing which was similar to the Rudra Tandavam of Sri Shiva.

समझ गए सब लोग कि कोई, भक्त पड़ा संकट में
क्षुभित खड़े थे सभी वहां पर पड़े हुए विस्मय में

Samajh gaye sab log ki koi,
bhakt pada sankat mein
Kshubhit khade the sabhi vaha
par pade huye vismay me

The entire gathering of the persons there had fathomed that an ardent devotee of Shri Sai Baba was in some difficulty and danger. The people seeing Shri Sai Baba had stood rooted there in complete silence overwhelmed by His grace.

उसे बचाने के ही खातिर, बाबा आज विकल हैं
उसकी ही पीड़ा से पीड़ित, उनका अन्त:स्थल है

Use bachane ki hi khatir,
Baba aaj vikal hain
uski hi peeda se peedit,
unka antah sthal hai

Shri Sai Baba was so much disturbed that day sensing the need to protect the devotee who was in trouble and danger. Shri Sai Baba's heart was so benevolent that He was anguished by the pain suffered by His devotee.

इतने में ही विधि ने अपनी, विचित्रता दिखलाई
देख कर जिसको जनता की, श्रद्धा-सरिता लहराई

Itne mein hi vidhi ne apni,
vichitrita dikhlai
dekh kar jisko janta ki,
shraddha-sarita lehrai

At that time, the providence had proved its wonderful nature. Seeing the anguish of Shri Sai Baba on the suffering of His devotee, the people near Him were flooded with the feeling of ardent devotion.

लेकर संज्ञाहीन भक्त को गाड़ी एक वहां आई
सम्मुख अपने देख भक्त को साईं की आंखें भर आईं

*Lekar sangyaheen bhakt
ko gaadi ek vaha aai
sammukh apne dekh bhakt ko
Sai ki aankhen bhar aayi*

A vehicle carrying the unconscious Kashi was brought to Shri Sai Baba. On seeing the condition of His devotee, Shri Sai Baba's eyes were tear filled.

शान्त धीर गम्भीर सिन्धु-सा बाबा का अन्तःस्थल
आज न जाने क्यों रह-रह कर हो जाता था चंचल

Shaant dheer gambhir
Sindhu sa baba ka antah sthal
aaj na jaane kyon
reh reh kar ho jata tha chanchal

Shri Sai Baba's soul was always calm, strong and was like ocean. However, that day it was turbulent with anxiety and sorrow over the condition of His devotee.

आज दया की मूर्ति स्वयं था, बना हुआ उपचारी
और भक्त के लिए आज था, देव बना प्रतिहारी

*Aaj daya ki moorti swayam tha,
bana hua upchari
aur bhakt ke liye aaj tha,
dev bana pratihari*

Today, Shri Sai Baba, the divine form Himself had become a doctor for His sincere devotee. The kind God had become the reliever of pain.

आज भक्ति की विषम परीक्षा में, सफल हुआ था 'काशी'
उसके ही दर्शन के खातिर, थे उमड़े नगर-निवासी

*Aaj bhakti ki visham pariksha mein,
safal hua tha 'Kashi'
uske hi darshan ke khatir,
the umde nagar-nivasi*

Kashi, the ardent devotee of Shri Sai Baba had succeeded in the difficult test of his devotion. The people of the town had arrived together to get his darshan.

जब भी और जहां भी कोई, भक्त पड़े संकट में
उसकी रक्षा करने बाबा, आते हैं पलभर में

Jab bhi aur jahaan bhi koi,
bhakt pade sankat mein
uski raksha karne baba,
aate hain palbhar mein

Shri Sai Baba appears instantly to protect His ardent devotees as and when the said devotees get into any difficulty and trouble.

युग-युग का है सत्य यह, नहीं कोई नई कहानी
आपात ग्रस्त भक्त जब होता, आते खुद अन्तर्यामी

*Yug-yug ka ha satya yeh,
nahin koi nai kahani
aapaat grast bhakt jab hota,
aate khud antaryami.*

Shri Sai Baba always rescues His sincere devotees whenever they face problems. This is not new.

भेद-भाव से परे पुजारी, मानवता के थे साईं
जितने प्यारे हिन्दु-मुस्लिम, उतने ही थे सिख ईसाई

Bhed-bhaav se pare pujaari,
maanavta ke the Sai
jitne pyaare Hindu-Muslim,
utne hi Sikh-Isaai

Shri Sai Baba does not discriminate. He is for the humanity as a whole. He has showered compassion on Hindus, Muslims, Sikhs and others equally.

भेद-भाव मन्दिर-मस्जिद का, तोड़-फोड़ बाबा ने डाला
राम-रहीम सभी उनके थे, कृष्ण-करीम-अल्लाहताला

Bhed bhaav mandir masjid ka,
tod-fod Baba ne daal
Ram-Rahim sabhi unke the,
Krishna-Karim-Allahtala

Shri Sai Baba had dimished the discrimination amongst religions whether it is a temple or a masjid. Both Ram and Rahim, Krishna, Karim and Allah belong to Shri Sai Baba.

घण्टे की प्रतिध्वनि से गूंजा, मस्जिद का कोना-कोना
मिले परस्पर हिन्दू-मुस्लिम, प्यार बढ़ा दिन-दिन दूना

Ghante ki pratidhvani se goonja,
Masjid ka kona-kona
mile paraspar Hindu-Muslim,
pyaar badha din-din doona

The reverberated sound of the bell echoed in the corners of the mosque. Both the Hindus and the Muslims gather there and meet each other. Their mutual cordiality gets multifold by the day.

चमत्कार था कितना सुंदर, परिचय इस काया ने दी
और नीम कड़ुवाहट में भी, मिठास बाबा ने भर दी

Chamatkar tha kitna sundar,
parichay iss kaya ne di
aur neem kaduvaahat mein bhi,
mithas Baba ne bhar di

This unity among people is so magically beautiful to consider. This amicability is introduced to this world by Shri Sai Baba as the God. With the blessings of Shri Sai Baba, even the bitter neem leaves get filled with sweetness.

सबको स्नेह दिया साईं ने, सबको सन्तुल प्यार किया
जो कुछ जिसने भी चाहा, बाबा ने उनको वही दिया

Sabko sneh diya Sai ne,
sabko santul pyar kiya
jo kuch jisne bhi chaha,
Baba ne usko wahi diya

Shri Sai Baba showers His love and blessings to all equally. Whatever His devotees aspire for, Shri Sai Baba surely grants the same.

ऐसे स्नेह शील भाजन का, नाम सदा जो जपा करे
पर्वत जैसा दुःख न क्यों हो, पलभर में वह दूर करे

Aise sneh sheel bhaajan ka,
naam sada jo japa kare
parvat jaisa dukh na kyon ho,
palbhar mein vah door kare

Shri Sai Baba is the saint full of love and compassion. To the person who recites His name constantly, even the worries and sadness in the size of the mountain shall wither away with the His blessings.

साईं जैसा दाता हमने, अरे नहीं देखा कोई
जिसके केवल दर्शन से ही, सारी विपदा दूर हो गई

Sai jaisa daata humne,
are nahin dekha koi
jiske keval darsha se hi,
saari vipda door ho gayi

Shri Sai Baba is so compassionate towards His devotees. Even the simple darshan of Him dissolves all the worries and pains.

तन में साईं, मन में साईं,
साईं-साईं भजा करो
अपने तन की सुधि-बुधि खोकर,
सुधि उसकी तुम किया करो

Tan mein Sai, mann mein Sai,
Sai-Sai bhaja karo
apne tan ki suddhi-buddhi khokar,
sudhi uski tum kiya karo

Shri Sai Baba is filled in our mind, body and soul. Do keep chanting 'Sai, Sai.' You leave being aware of your body. You concentrate and meditate solely on Shri Sai Baba.

जब तू अपनी सुधि तज, बाबा की सुधि किया करेगा
और रात-दिन बाबा, बाबा ही तू रटा करेगा

Jab tu apni sudhi taj,
Baba kiya sudhi kiya karega
aur raat-din Baba,
Baba hi tu rata karega

Once you cease to think of yourself and commence meditating on Shri Sai Baba, during day and night, you will be only reciting 'Baba, Baba' all the time.

तो बाबा को अरे! विवश हो, सुधि तेरी लेनी ही होगी
तेरी हर इच्छा बाबा को, पूरी ही करनी होगी

To Baba ko are! vivash ho,
Sudhi teri leni hi hogi
Teri har iccha Baba ko,
poori hi karni hogi

With your unending chanting of Shri Sai Baba, He will surely pay attention to you and He will consider all your wishes and will fulfill your every wish.

जंगल-जंगल भटक न पागल, और ढूंढ़ने बाबा को
एक जगह केवल शिर्डी में, तू पायेगा बाबा को

Jungle-jungle bhatak na pagal,
aur dhoondhane Baba ko
ek jagah keval Shirdi mein,
tu payega Baba ko

Oh ignorant mind! abstain from wandering from place to place in search of Shri Sai Baba. You will find Him only in Shirdi.

धन्य जगत में प्राणी है वह, जिसने बाबा को पाया
दु:ख में सुख में प्रहर आठ हो, साई का ही गुण गाया

Dhanya jagat mein praani hai vah,
jisne Baba ko paaya
dukh me sukh main prahar aath ho,
Sai ka hi gun gaya

The devotee of Shri Sai Baba who has obtained refuge in Him is blessed. In happiness, in sadness and in the eight phases of each day, he only praises the name of Shri Sai Baba.

गिरे संकटों के पर्वत, चाहे बिजली ही टूट पड़े
साईं का ले नाम सदा तुम, सम्मुख सब के रहो अड़े

Gire sankaton ke parvat,
chahe bijli hi toot pade
Saika ka le naam sada tum,
sammukh sab ke raho ade

The devotee remembering the name of Shri Sai Baba can face all the troubles bravely even if there is striking of lightning. All his mountain of troubles will fade away with the blessings of Shri Sai Baba.

इस बूढ़े की करामात सुन, तुम हो जाओगे हैरान
दंग रह गये सुनकर जिसको, जाने कितने चतुर सुजान

iss boodhe ki karamat sun,
tum ho jaoge hairan
dang reh gaye sunkar jisko,
jaane kitne chatur sujaan.

The persons who listen to this story of the old man will be dumbstruck with shock. Many intelligent people were shocked at the story.

एक बार शिर्डी में साधू, ढ़ोंगी था कोई आया
भोली-भाली नगर-निवासी, जनता को था भरमाया

Ek baar Shirdi mein saadhu,
dhongee tha koi aaya
bholi-bhali nagar-nivasi,
janta ko tha bharmaya

Long back, Shirdi was visited by a person who appeared as a Sadhu and he was a cheat. Innocent residents of the town were misguided by him.

जड़ी-बूटियां उन्हें दिखाकर, करने लगा वहां भाषण
कहने लगा सुनो श्रोतागण, घर मेरा है वृन्दावन

*Jadi-bootiyan unhe dikhakar,
karne laga vahan bhaashan
kehne laga suno shrotagan,
ghar mera hai Vrindavan*

The Sadhu had showed various types of herbs to the residents and told them 'listen to me; My home is in Vrindhavan.'

औषधि मेरे पास एक है, और अजब इसमें शक्ति
इसके सेवन करने से ही, हो जाती दुःख से मुक्ति

Aushadhi mere pass ek hai,
aur ajab ismein shakti
iske sevan karne se hi,
ho jaati dukh se mukti

I have an unique healing medicine with me; It has wonderful powers; The dosage and usage of this medicine alleviates all pains and worries.

अगर मुक्त होना चाहो तुम, संकट से बीमारी से
तो है मेरा नम्र निवेदन, हर नर से हर नारी से

Agar mukt hona chaho tum,
sankat se bimari se
to hai mera namra nivedan,
har nar se har naari se

Oh the men and women here, if you wish to be free of worries and ailments, this is my most humble request to you.

लो खरीद तुम इसको इसकी, सेवन विधियां हैं न्यारी
यद्यपि तुच्छ वस्तु है यह, गुण उसके हैं अति भारी

Lo khareed tum isko iski,
sevan vidhiyan hai nyaari
yadyapi tucchh vastu hai yeh
gun uske hai ati bhari

You people come forward and get this medicine; Though it looks trivial, there are unique benefits in its usage and the results are enormous.

जो है संतति हीन यहां यदि, मेरी औषधि को खायें
पुत्र-रत्न हो प्राप्त, अरे वह मुंह मांगा फल पायें

*Jo hai santan heen yaha yadi,
meri aushadhi ko khayein
putra-ratna ho prapt,
are vah mooh maanga phal paaye*

In case there is a person without progeny here, that person can have this medicine. That person shall be bestowed with progeny and the other wishes shall also be fulfilled.

औषधि मेरी जो न खरीदे, जीवन भर पछतायेगा
मुझ जैसा प्राणी शायद ही, अरे यहां आ पायेगा

Aushadhi meri jo na khareede,
jeevan bhar pachtayega
mujh jaisa prani shayad hi,
are yahan aa paayega

The persons who do not get the medicine from me will regret their folly for the rest of their lives. It is unlikely that a person like me visits this place again.

दुनिया दो दिन का मेला है, मौज शौक तुम भी कर लो
गर इससे मिलता है, सब कुछ तुम भी इसको ले लो

Duniya do din ka mela hai,
mauj shauk tum bhi kar lo
gar iss se milta hai,
sab kuch tum bhi isko lelo

The world is like the show of exhibition lasting for two days. You must enjoy and fulfill your desires to the possible extent. If you buy the miracle medicine from me, your wishes will be fulfilled.

हैरानी बढ़ती जनता की देख इसकी कारस्तानी
प्रमुदित वह भी मन ही मन था, देख लोगों की नादानी

Hairani badhti janta ki
dekh iski karasthani
pramudit vah bhi man hi man tha,
dekh logon ki naadaani

The people who had listened to his claims were awestruck with his speech and actions. The Sadhu was also gratified to see the large crowd of simple, ignorant and innocent people.

खबर सुनाने बाबा को यह, गया दौड़कर सेवक एक
सुनकर भृकुटि तनी और, विस्मरण हो गया सभी विवेक

Khabar sunane Baba ko yeh,
gaya daudkar sevak ek
sunkar bhrikuti tanee aur,
vismaran ho gaya sabhi vivek

One of the devotees of Shri Sai Baba ran to him to tell about the news of the Sadhu. Shri Sai Baba was surprised and perturbed. His sense of calm was shattered.

हुक्म दिया सेवक को, सत्वर पकड़ दुष्ट को लाओ
या शिर्डी की सीमा से, कपटी को दूर भगाओ

Hukum diya sevak ko,
satvar pakad drishti ko laao
ya Shirdi ki seema se,
kapti ko door bhagao

Shri Sai Baba had ordered His followers to either bring the cheating Sadhu to Him or to forcefully drive the Sadhu away from the borders of Shirdi.

मेरे रहते भोली-भाली, शिर्डी की जनता को
कौन नीच ऐसा जो, साहस करता है छलने को

Mere rehte bholi-bhali,
Shirdi ki janta ko
kaun neech aisa jo,
sahas karta hai chhalne ko

Shri Sai Baba said, 'as long as I am here, I will not allow the innocent people of Shirdi being cheated by this lowly person.'

पल भर में ही ऐसे ढ़ोंगी, कपटी नीच लुटेरे को
महानाश के महागर्त में, पहुंचा दूं जीवन भर को

Pal bhar mein hi aise dhongi,
kapti neech lootere ko
mahanash ke mahagarth mein,
pahuncha doon jeevan bhar ko

I will subject this lowly being who is a cheat, hypocrite and thief to the worst form of diminution. He will suffer for the rest of his life.

तनिक मिला आभास मदारी क्रूर कुटिल अन्यायी को
काल नाचता है अब सिर पर गुस्सा आया साईं को

*Tanik mila aabhaas madari
kroor kutil anyayi ko
kaal naachta hai ab
sir par gussa aya Sai ko*

Shri Sai Baba was enraged with his actions. He said, 'I wish to see this cruel and crooked magician. His time is hovering above his head.'

पल भर में सब खेल बन्द कर भागा सिर पर रखकर पैर
सोच था मन ही मन, भगवान नहीं है अब खैर

Pal bhar main sab khel band kar
bhaaga sir par rakh kar pair
socha tha mann hi mann,
bhagwan nahin hai ab khair

At the same time, the cheat Sadhu had a feeling that he could escape from the punishment of the God. So he stopped his cheating work and ran to flee from the town.

सच है साईं जैसा दानी, मिल न सकेगा जग में
अंश ईश का साईंबाबा, उन्हें न कुछ भी मुश्किल जग में

Sach hai Sai jaisa daanee,
mil na sakega jag mein
ansh Eish ka Sai Baba,
unhein na kuch bhi mushkil jag mein

The benefactor like Shri Sai Baba cannot be found anywhere in the universe. When Shri Sai Baba blesses and be with the devotee, nothing in the world is tough for the devotee.

स्नेह, शील, सौजन्य आदि का, आभूषण धारण कर
बढ़ता इस दुनिया में जो भी, मानव-सेवा के पथ पर

Sneh, sheel, saujanya, aadi ka,
aabhushan dhaaran kar
badhta is duniya mein jo bhi,
manav-seva ke path par

When a person wishes to progress in the world in the path of service to humanity, he adorns, friendliness, humility, affection and kindness as ornaments.

वही जीत लेता है जगती के, जन-जन का अन्तःस्थल
उसकी एक उदासी ही जग को कर देती है विह्वल

Vahi jeet leta hai jagti ke,
jan-jan ka antahsthal
uski ek udasi hi
jag ko kar deti hai vihval

Shri Sai Baba is the one who is prevailing over the universe. He exists in the souls of all the beings. If He Himself is saddened even a little, it will cripple the world.

जब-जब जग में भार पाप का, बढ़ बढ़ ही जाता है
उसे मिटाने के ही खातिर, अवतारी ही आता है

Jab jab jag main bhaar paap ka,
badh badh hi jaata hai
use mitane ke hi khatir,
avtari hi aata hai

As and when the sins in the world get too heavy beyond endurance, Lord Sri Maha Vishnu takes an incarnation to diminish those sins.

पाप और अन्याय सभी कुछ, इस जगती का हर के
दूर भगा देता दुनिया के, दानव को क्षण भर में

Paap aur anyay sabhi kuch,
iss jagati ka har ke
door bhaga deta hai duniya ke,
daanav ko kshan bhar mein

The said incarnation of Sri Maha Vishu destroys and dissolves all the sins and injustice in the world. All the demons flee away in His presence.

स्नेह सुधा की धार बरसने, लगती है इस दुनिया में
गले परस्पर मिलने लगते, जन-जन आपस में

Sneh sudha ki dhaar barasne,
lagti hai iss duniya mein
gale paraspar milne lagte,
jan-jan aapas mein

The showers of nectar from the God and love commence descending on this world. The devotees started embracing themselves with affection among themselves.

ऐसे ही अवतारी साईं, मृत्युलोक में आकर
समता का यह पाठ पढ़ाया, सबको अपना आप मिटाकर

Aise hi avtari Sai,
mrityulok mein aakar
samta ka yah path padhaya,
sabko apna aap mitakar

Shri Sai Baba is such incarnation who was born in this world. He had taught the lesson of peaceful co-existence and sense of equality by not giving consideration to selfish interests.

नाम द्वारका मस्जिद का, रक्खा शिर्डी में साईं ने
दाप, ताप, सन्ताप मिटाया, जो कुछ आया साईं ने

Naam Dwarka masjid ka,
rakha Shirdi mein Sai ne
daap, taap, suntaap mitaya,
jo kuch aaya Sai ne

At Shirdi, Shri Sai Baba had called a mosque as Dwaraka making it similar to the birthplace of Sri Krishna. He had removed anger, illness, worries, troubles and other problems.

सदा याद में मस्त राम की, बैठे रहते थे साईं
पहर आठ ही राम नाम का, भजते रहते थे साईं

Sada yaad mein mast Ram ki,
baithe rehte the Sai,
peher aath hi Ram naam ka,
bhajte rehte the Sai

Shri Sai Baba constantly is in meditation with the lovely thoughts and chants of Lord Sri Ram in all the eight phases of the day.

सूखी-रूखी, ताजी-बासी, चाहे या होवे पकवान
सदा प्यार के भूखे साईं की, खातिर थे सभी समान

Sookhi rookhi, taji baasi,
chaahe ya hove pakwaan
sada pyaar ke bhukhe Sai ki,
khatir the sabhi sammaan

Shri Sai Baba had hunger only for love and compassion. To Him, all food, be it fresh, stale, dried, or withered, is equally sacred.

स्नेह और श्रद्धा से अपनी, जन जो कुछ दे जाते थे
बड़े चाव से उस भोजन को, बाबा पावन करते थे

Sneh aur shraddha se apni.
jan jo kuch de jaate the
bade chaav se us bhojan ka,
baba paavan karte the

Shri Sai Baba always accepts any food offered by His devotees and eats the same with enthusiasm and makes it a blessed prasad.

कभी-कभी मन बहलाने को, बाबा बाग में जाते थे
प्रमुदित मन निरख प्रकृति, छटा के वे होते थे

*Kabhi kabhi mann bahlaane ko,
Baba baag mein jaate the
pramudit man nirakh prakriti,
chhata ke ve hote the*

Shri Sai Baba at times visits the garden and observes the nature. It calms His mind and it makes Him happy.

रंग-बिरंगे पुष्प बाग के, मन्द-मन्द हिल-डुल करके
बीहड़ वीराने मन में भी, स्नेह सलिल भर जाते थे

Rang-birange pushp baag ke,
mand-mand hil-dul karke
beehad virane mann mein bhi,
sneh salil bhar jaate the

The flowers in the garden which are full of colours used to sway as if in a trance. The sight of those shall bring love and compassion even to the silent and peaceful mind.

ऐसी सुमधुर बेला में भी, दुःख आपात विपदा के मारे
अपने मन की व्यथा सुनाने, जन रहते बाबा को घेरे

Aise sumdhur bela mein bhi,
dukh aapaat vipda ke maare
apne mann ki vyattha sunane,
jan rehte baba ko ghere

Shri Sai Baba is surrounded by people who are tortured, afflicted with worries, sadness and troubles who pour in their woes to Him.

सुनकर जिनकी करूण कथा को, नयन कमल भर आते थे
दे विभूति हर व्यथा, शान्ति, उनके उर में भर देते थे

Sunkar jinkee karun katha ko,
nayan kamal bhar aate the
de vibhooti har vyatha, shanti,
unke ur me bhar dete the

Shri Sai Baba used to fill His eyes with tears whenever He heard the sadness from His devotees. He gave them the sacred ash thereby alleviating their pains and fill them with peace of mind.

जाने क्या अद्भुत, शक्ति, उस विभूति में होती थी
जो धारण करते मस्तक पर, दुःख सारा हर लेती थी

Jaane kya adbhut shakti,
uss vibhuti mein hoti thi
jo dhaaran karte mastak par,
dukh sara har leti thi

It is really wonderful that once the holy ash is applied on one's forehead, all the worries and sadness wither away.

धन्य मनुज वे साक्षात् दर्शन, जो बाबा साईं के पाये
धन्य कमल-कर उनके जिनसे, चरण-कमल वे परसाये

*Dhanya manuja veh saakshaath
dharshan, jo baba Sai kae paayae
Dhanya kamal-kar unke jinsae
charan-kamal veh parsaye*

The people who get the darshan of Shri Sai Baba are blessed. Of them, those who had the chance to touch the holy feet of Shri Sai Baba are very much blessed.

काश निर्भय तुमको भी, साक्षात साईं मिल जाता
बरसों से उजड़ा चमन अपना, फिर से आज खिल जाता

Kaash nirbhay tumko bhi,
saakshaat Sai mil jata
barson se ujda chaman apna,
phir se aaj khil jata

Getting the blessings of Shri Sai Baba makes you fearless. His blessings turn your life from a dried up land to a blooming colourful garden.

गर पकड़ता मैं चरण श्री के, नहीं छोड़ता उम्रभर
मना लेता मैं जरूर उनको, गर रूठते साईं मुझ पर

Gar pakadta main charan Shri ke,
nahin chodhta umra bhar
manaa leta main zaroor unko,
gar roothte Sai mujh par

I shall hold the holy feet of Shri Sai Baba and I will never leave them for my life. Even if I have done something to anger Him, by steadfastly holding His feet, I will be able to make Him forgive me.

श्री साईं बाबा आरती

आरती श्री साईं गुरुवर की, परमानन्द सदा सुरवर की।
जा की कृपा विपुल सुखकारी, दुःख शोक, संकट भयहारी ॥

आरती श्री साईं गुरुवर की, परमानन्द सदा सुरवर की।

शिरडी में अवतार रचाया, चमत्कार से तत्व दिखाया।
कितने भक्त चरण पर आये, वे सुख शान्ति चिरंतन पाये॥

आरती श्री साईं गुरुवर की, परमानन्द सदा सुरवर की।

भाव धरै जो मन में जैसा, पावत अनुभव वो ही वैसा।
गुरु की उदी लगावे तन को, समाधान लाभत उस मन को॥

आरती श्री साईं गुरुवर की, परमानन्द सदा सुरवर की।

साईं नाम सदा जो गावे, सो फल जग में शाश्वत पावे।
गुरुवासर करि पूजा-सेवा, उस पर कृपा करत गुरुदेवा ॥

आरती श्री साईं गुरुवर की, परमानन्द सदा सुरवर की।

राम, कृष्ण, हनुमान रुप में, दे दर्शन, जानत जो मन में।
विविध धर्म के सेवक आते, दर्शन कर इच्छित फल पाते।।

आरती श्री साईं गुरुवर की, परमानन्द सदा सुरवर की।

जै बोलो साईं बाबा की, जै बोलो अवधूत गुरु की।
'साईंदास' आरती को गावै, घर में बसि सुख, मंगल पावे।।

आरती श्री साईं गुरुवर की, परमानन्द सदा सुरवर की।

Aarti Sai Baba

Aarti Shri Sai Guruvar Ki,
Paramananda Sada Suravar Ki ।
Ja Ki Kripa Vipula Sukhakari,
Dukh Shok, Sankat, Bhayahari ॥

Aarti Shri Sai Guruvar Ki,
Paramananda Sada Suravar Ki ।

Shirdi Mein Avatar Rachaya,
Chamatkar Se Tatva Dikhaya ।
Kitane Bhakt Charana Par Aye,
Ve Sukh Shanti Chirantan Paye ॥

Aarti Shri Sai Guruvar Ki,
Paramananda Sada Suravar Ki ।

Bhaav Dhare Jo Mana Me Jaisa,
Pavat Anubhav Vo Hi Vaisa ।
Guru Ki Udi Lagave Tann Ko,
Samadhan Labhat Us Mann Ko ॥

Aarti Shri Sai Guruvar Ki,
Paramananda Sada Suravar Ki ।

Sai Nama Sada Jo Gave,
So Phal Jag Mein Shashvat Pave ।
Guruvasara Kari Puja Seva,
Us Par Kripa Karata Gurudeva ॥

Aarti Shri Sai Guruvar Ki,
Paramanand Sada Suravar Ki ।

Rama, Krishna, Hanuman Roop Mein,
De Darshan, Janata Jo Mann Mein ।
Vividha Dharm Ke Sevak Ate,
Darshan Kar Ichchhit Phal Pate ॥

Aarti Shri Sai Guruvar Ki,
Paramananda Sada Suravar Ki ।

Jai Bolo Sai Baba Ki,
Jai Bolo Avadhut Guru Ki ।
'Saidas' Aarti Ko Gave, Ghar Mein Basi
Sukha, Mangala Pave ॥

Aarti Shri Sai Guruvar Ki,
Paramananda Sada Suravar Ki ॥

Aarti Sai Baba

Aarti of Shri Sai, the Revered Guru,
Eternal Bliss to the Celestial Lord.

Whose grace brings immense joy,
Dispelling sorrow, grief, troubles, and fear.

Aarti of Shri Sai, the Revered Guru,
Eternal Bliss to the Celestial Lord.

He incarnated in Shirdi,
Revealed the truth through miracles.

Countless devotees came to his feet,
And received eternal peace and happiness.

Aarti of Shri Sai, the Revered Guru,
Eternal Bliss to the Celestial Lord.

Whatever feeling one holds in the heart,
That exact experience they receive.

Applying the sacred ash (Udi) to the body,
Brings peace and fulfillment to the mind.

Aarti of Shri Sai, the Revered Guru,
Eternal Bliss to the Celestial Lord.

One who always chants Sai's name,
Attains eternal reward in this world.

Worshipping and serving
the Guru with devotion,
Receives the Guru's divine blessings.

Aarti of Shri Sai, the Revered Guru,
Eternal Bliss to the Celestial Lord.

In the forms of Ram,
Krishna, and Hanuman,
He appears to those
who truly believe.

Devotees of all religions come,
And get their wishes fulfilled
by his darshan (divine vision).

Aarti of Shri Sai, the Revered Guru,
Eternal Bliss to the Celestial Lord.

Glory to Sai Baba!
Glory to the Avadhut Guru!

'Sai Das' sings this Aarti,
May peace and auspiciousness
reside in his home.

Aarti of Shri Sai, the Revered Guru,
Eternal Bliss to the Celestial Lord.